I0541246

www.ingramcontent.com/pod-product-compliance
Lightning Source LLC
Chambersburg PA
CBHW041539120626
46551CB00019B/2762

* 9 7 9 8 9 9 2 1 6 9 3 1 7 *

THIS WORKBOOK BELONGS TO

....

....

....

....

Hebrew 2 Workbook: Learn to Write the Hebrew Cursive Script Alphabet – For Kids and Adults – B&W Interior

2nd Edition

ISBN: 979-8-9921693-1-7

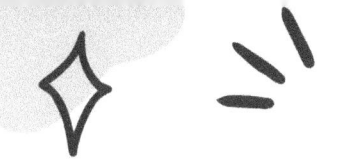

READY TO MASTER CURSIVE SCRIPT?

Welcome to your Hebrew 2 Workbook!

If you've completed Hebrew 1 Workbook — way to go! You're well on your way to confidently reading and writing Hebrew. Turn to the next page and let's make the most of Hebrew 2.

If you haven't taken Hebrew 1 Workbook yet, I highly recommend starting there. Hebrew 1 teaches you *everything* you need to write like a pro using **Print** letters — the ones you see everywhere, from books and subtitles to signs. My unique, step-by-step approach ensures you'll build a strong foundation for everything that comes next. Trust me — it'll make this step, Cursive Script, so much easier.

WHY CURSIVE SCRIPT?

In Israel, Cursive Script is how we handwrite. You'll also see it used in ads, menus, and signs - as a way to stand out. While you don't have to use it for your own writing, you'll *absolutely* need to recognize it — which is why this workbook is an essential step in completing *all* your reading and writing skills in Hebrew.

For best results, complete Hebrew 1 *before* diving into this workbook.

STEP 3: THE VOWEL NIKUD SYSTEM

Hebrew 1 & 2 complete all your *writing* skills, and Hebrew 3 completes your *reading* skills. It simplifies the Nikud vowel system — a topic that's challenging for most — but don't worry! My Hebrew 3 is all about making it practical, clear, and easy to understand.

Find all the ways to order Hebrew 1 Workbook & Hebrew 3 Textbook at **hebrewbyinbal.com/order**.

Wherever you're starting from, I'm thrilled to guide you through this step. Let's go!

Your excited Hebrew teacher,

UNLOCK THE FULL VALUE OF YOUR WORKBOOK

Unlock Your Free Course
Hebrew 2 workbook comes with a free course! Inside, I'll guide you step by step through the workbook, give you extra practice, you'll master my proprietary phonetic system used in this workbook, access my direct support, and build your confidence every step of the way.

Enroll for free at **learn.hebrewbyinbal.com/2348** and unlock a comprehensive learning experience.

Designed for All Ages
Hebrew 1 and 2 are perfect for all ages! If you're a young learner, ask an adult to help you with anything you're unsure about. Add color to each letter and illustration to make learning even more fun.

Your Roadmap to Success
The next page will show you all the treasures you'll find for each letter. Think of it as your roadmap to discovering the delights of this workbook.

Hebrew reading and writing is right to left
This workbook will help you adapt to this new style with ease. Helpful arrows and instructions are included throughout to guide you every step of the way.

Each letter is taught using familiar English words that we Israelis commonly use (a new set from Hebrew 1), written in Hebrew, English, and with my phonetic system that you master inside your free course.

Tracing Matters
Properly writing Hebrew letters starts with tracing. Follow the middle line of each letter, not its outline, and use the arrows and numbers provided for the correct sequence.

After tracing each letter or word, test your skills with freehand writing in the spaces provided. For extra practice, use a pencil to trace, erase, and trace again. Don't forget the extra practice pages at the end of your workbook.

A SAMPLE OF EACH LETTER PAGE

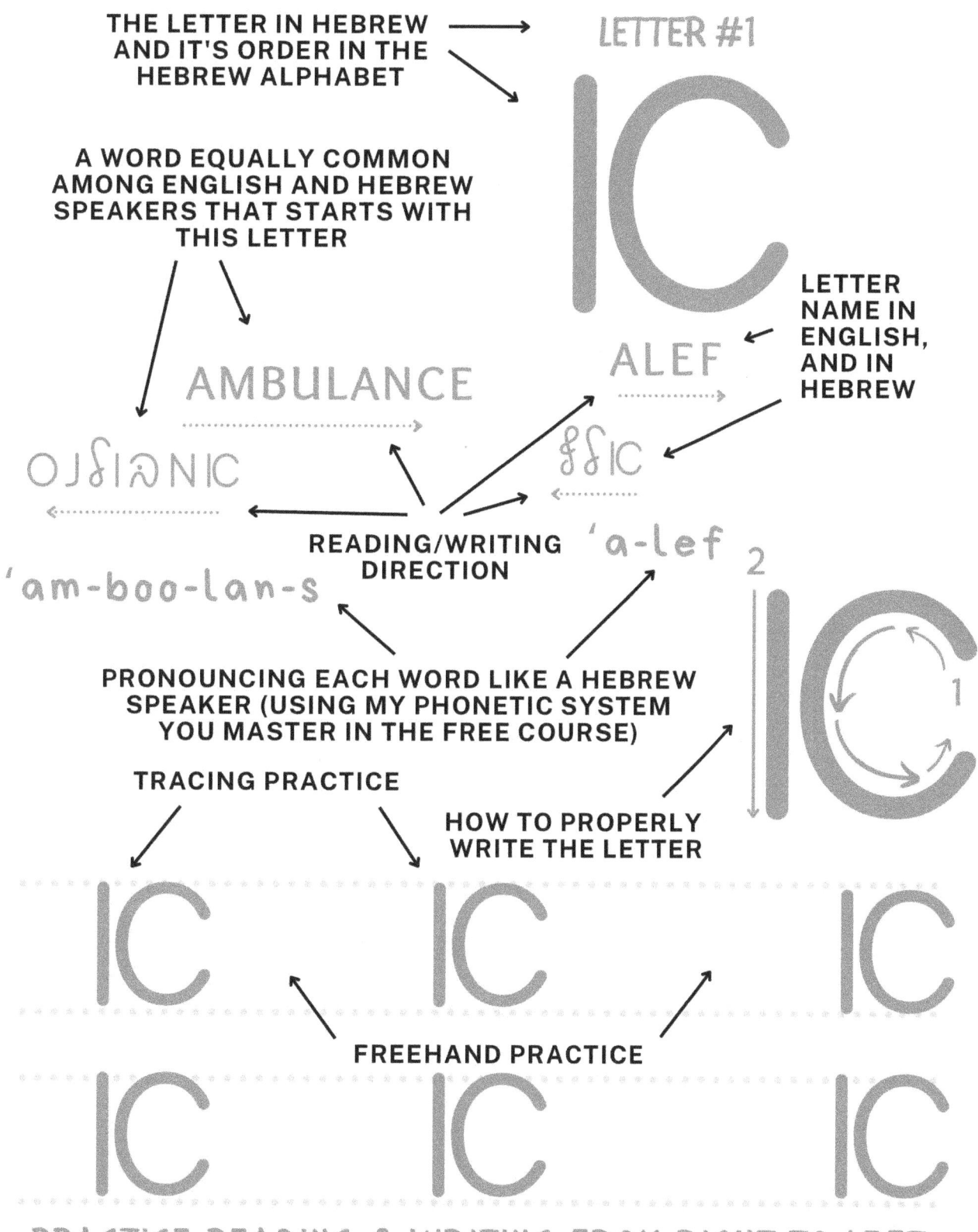

THE LETTER IN HEBREW AND IT'S ORDER IN THE HEBREW ALPHABET

LETTER #1

A WORD EQUALLY COMMON AMONG ENGLISH AND HEBREW SPEAKERS THAT STARTS WITH THIS LETTER

LETTER NAME IN ENGLISH, AND IN HEBREW

ALEF

AMBULANCE

READING/WRITING DIRECTION

'am-boo-lan-s

'a-lef

PRONOUNCING EACH WORD LIKE A HEBREW SPEAKER (USING MY PHONETIC SYSTEM YOU MASTER IN THE FREE COURSE)

TRACING PRACTICE

HOW TO PROPERLY WRITE THE LETTER

FREEHAND PRACTICE

PRACTICE READING & WRITING FROM RIGHT TO LEFT

HEY THERE!
I HOPE YOU'RE EXCITED

You're about to learn to write the hand-written form in Hebrew, called Cursive/Script

Now that you write so well in Print, I'm sure you will do just as great writing in Cursive / Script letters

What if I were to tell you that you know ANOTHER 20+ words in Hebrew?

Well, YOU DO! For each letter you will discover a new word you know how to say PERFECTLY in Hebrew

THINGS TO KNOW ABOUT LETTER SHAPES

Hebrew Cursive/Script letters look different from Print letters, with more curved lines, but they sound exactly the same

Letters have many styles and shapes (called fonts). This can be a bit confusing when you're just starting to learn the letters

That is why the letter shape (font) you'll learn here is a common, easy, and practical one

If the shape of the letter at the top of each page and the one at the bottom is not 100% the same, it's ok. I want you to see more than one font

IC

ALEF

ᴊᴊIC   'a-lef

AMBULANCE

OJᴊᴁᴑNIC

'am-boo-lan-s

2

IC   1

IC   IC   IC   IC

IC   IC   IC

PRACTICE READING & WRITING FROM RIGHT TO LEFT

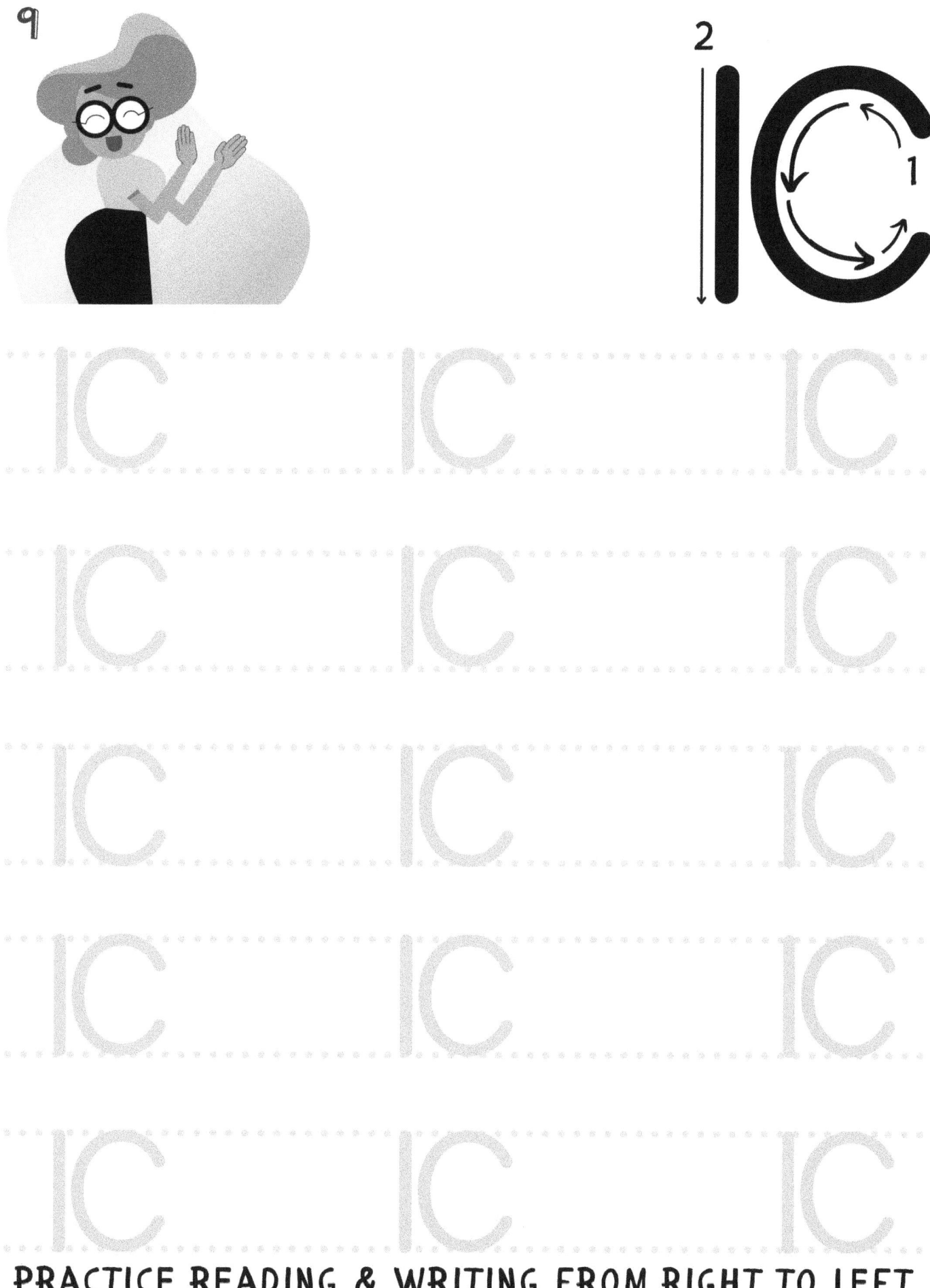

BET

בֵּית   bet

BAGEL

בּייגֶל

'bey-gel

PRACTICE READING & WRITING FROM RIGHT TO LEFT

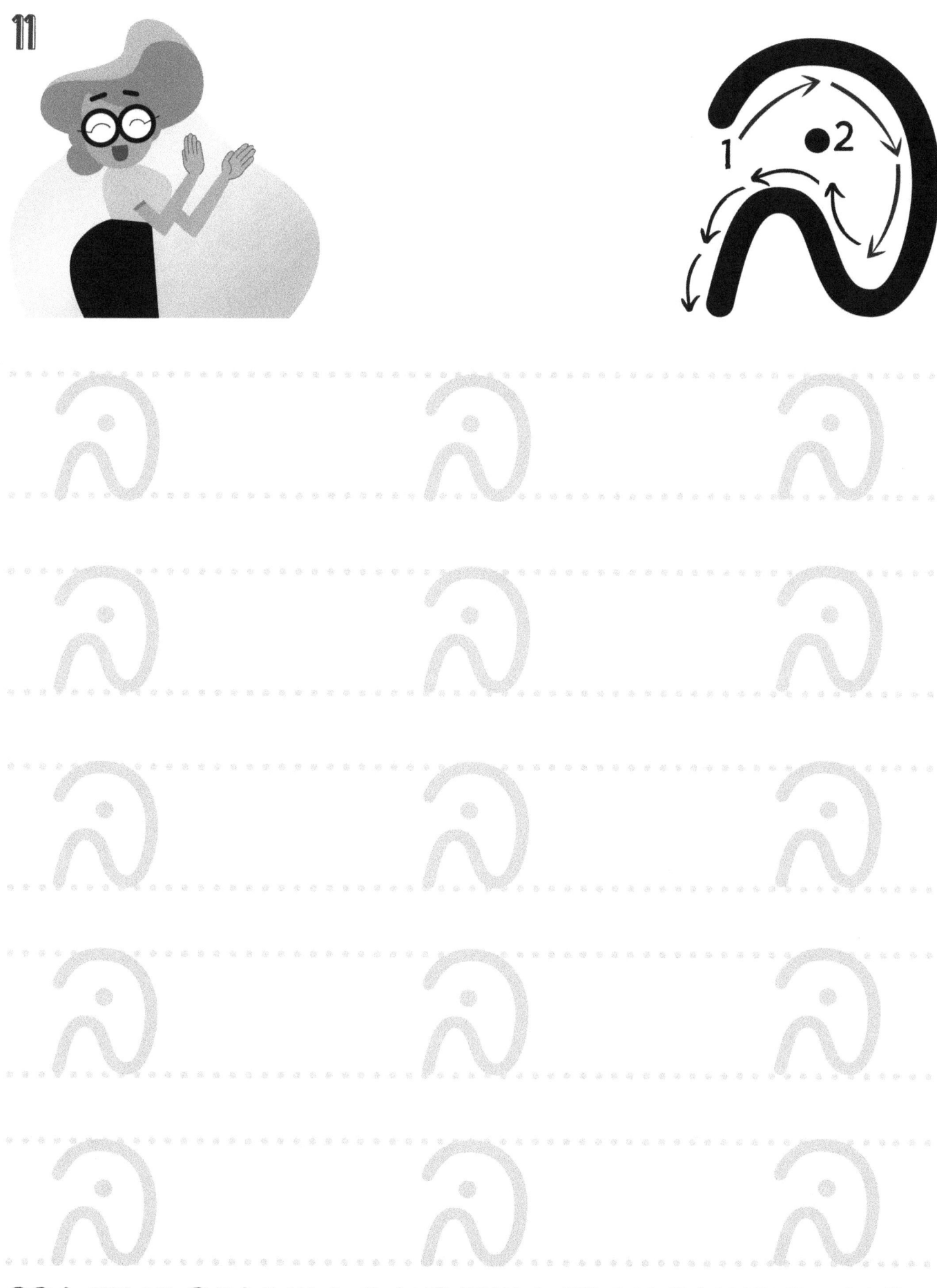

THINGS TO KNOW ABOUT

ב

BET

The letter Bet has a variation called Vet when you take off the dot in the middle

ב

VET

VET sounds like the English letter V as in the words Van and Vacation

There are 3 letters in Hebrew with and without a dot/Dugesh (pronounced da-gesh).

When these 3 letters have a dot, we say "With Dugesh". When it is removed, we say "No Dugesh".

We mark them with a heart.

BET becomes VET by taking off the dot (Dugesh) in the middle. This is how we write VET = BET with no Dugesh

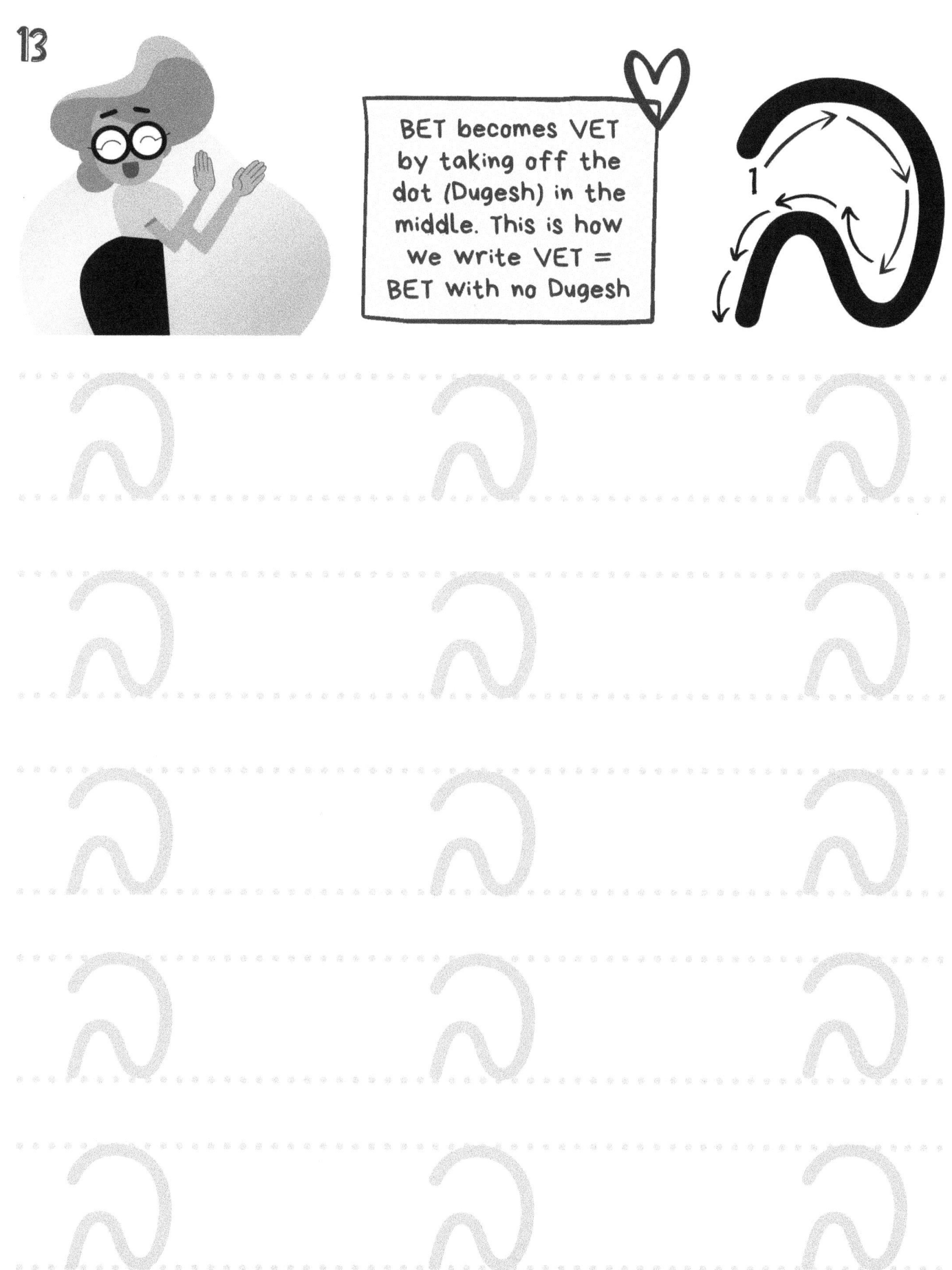

PRACTICE READING & WRITING FROM RIGHT TO LEFT

GUITAR

גִיטָרָה

gee-'ta-rah

GIMEL

גִּימֶל

'gee-mel

PRACTICE READING & WRITING FROM RIGHT TO LEFT

'ר

GIMEL ALWAYS MAKES A
SOUND AS IN THE WORD
GUITAR.
GIMEL WRITTEN WITH '
SIGN MAKES A SOUND AS
IS THE WORD GENTLE

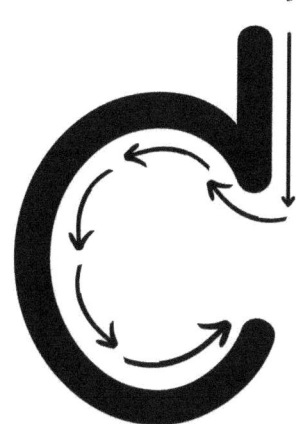

1

PRACTICE READING & WRITING FROM RIGHT TO LEFT

YOUR FIRST WORD IN HEBREW

let's put the 3rd letter
GIMEL twice
to write the word
ROOF in Hebrew:

גג

Say it in Hebrew: gag

גג   גג

PRACTICE READING & WRITING FROM RIGHT TO LEFT

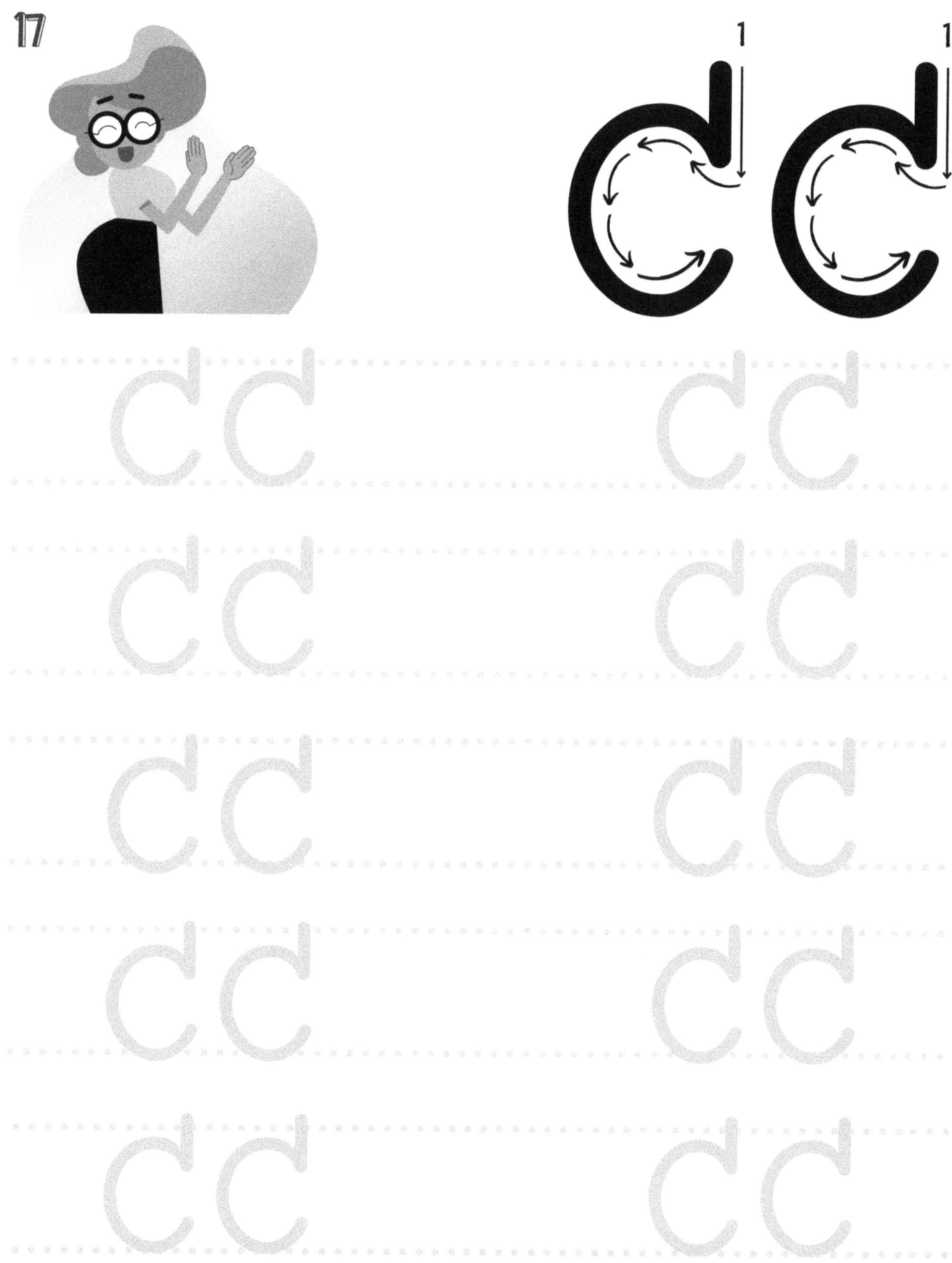

PRACTICE READING & WRITING FROM RIGHT TO LEFT

DALET

דלת

'da-let

DOLLAR

דולר

'do-lar

PRACTICE READING & WRITING FROM RIGHT TO LEFT

PRACTICE READING & WRITING FROM RIGHT TO LEFT

YOUR SECOND WORD IN HEBREW

Now let's put together the
4th letter DALET
and the Second letter VET
(no dot) to write the word
BEAR:

בד

Say it in Hebrew: dov

בד   בד

PRACTICE READING & WRITING FROM RIGHT TO LEFT

21

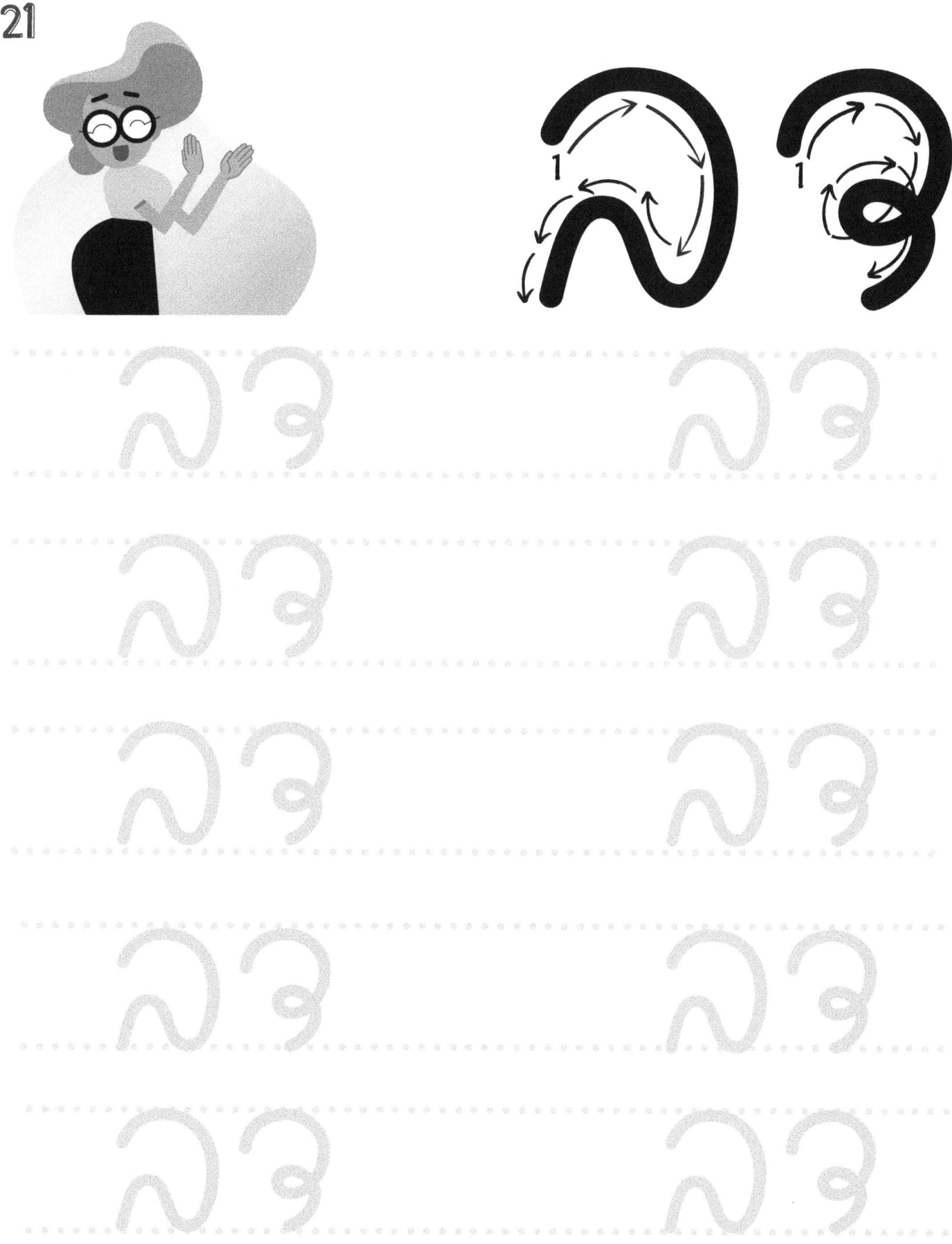

PRACTICE READING & WRITING FROM RIGHT TO LEFT

HE / HEY

············>

he / hey

HI

·····>

hay

PRACTICE READING & WRITING FROM RIGHT TO LEFT

23

PRACTICE READING & WRITING FROM RIGHT TO LEFT

VAV

VITAMIN

I'NGʻI

II

vav

1

vee-ta-'meen

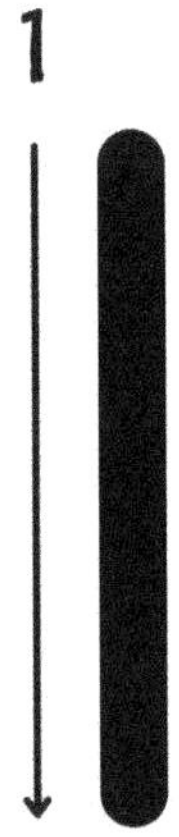

PRACTICE READING & WRITING FROM RIGHT TO LEFT

1

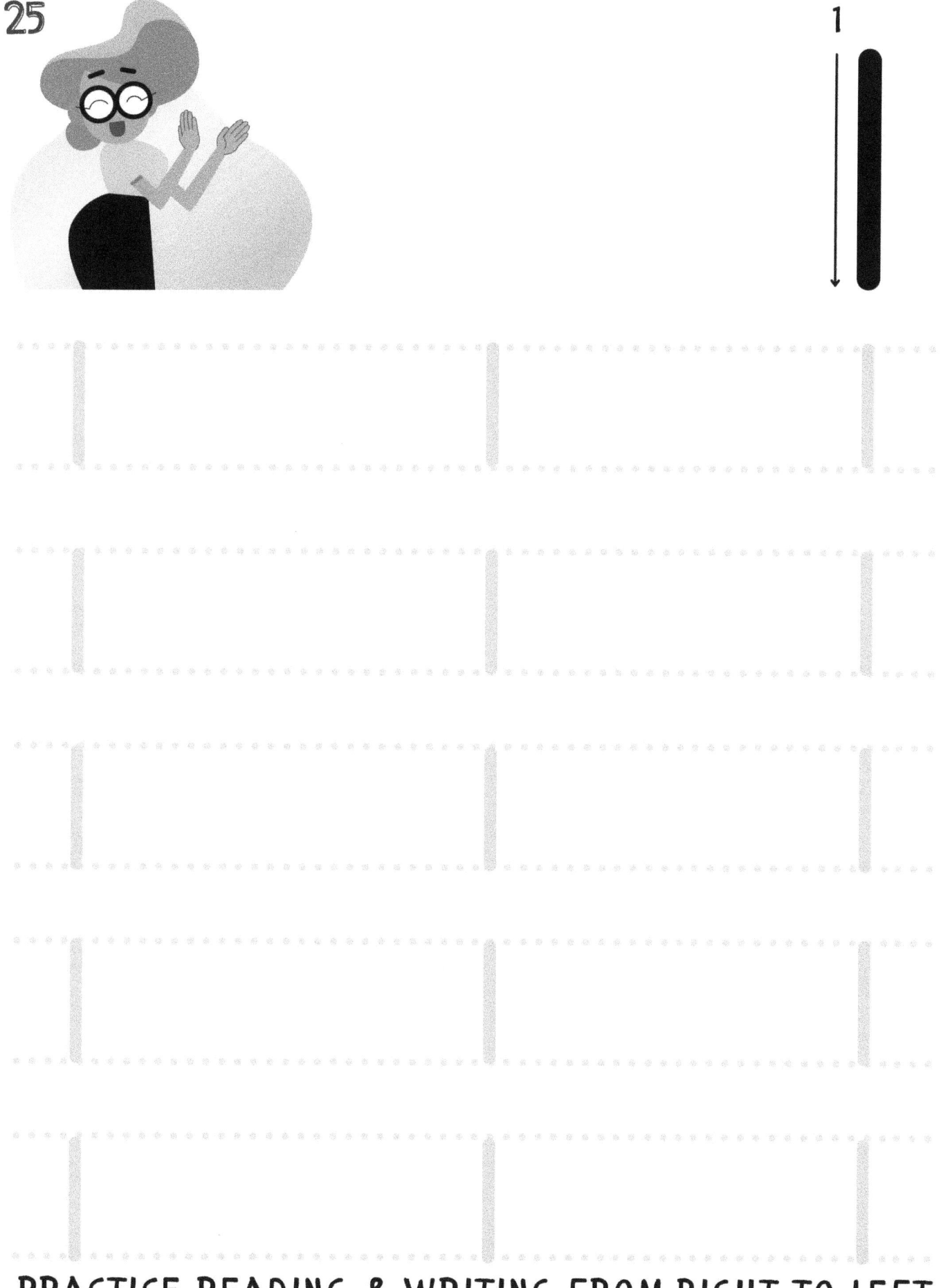

PRACTICE READING & WRITING FROM RIGHT TO LEFT

ZAYIN

'za-yeen

ן'ז

ZEBRA

ז'ברה

'zeb-rah

1

PRACTICE READING & WRITING FROM RIGHT TO LEFT

PRACTICE READING & WRITING FROM RIGHT TO LEFT

LETTER #8

ח

CHET / KHET

········→

חית khet

←········

CHALLAH

········→

חלה

←········

kha-'lah

2
1

ח

ח ח ח
ח ח ח

PRACTICE READING & WRITING FROM RIGHT TO LEFT

THINGS TO KNOW ABOUT

ח

KHET

KHET is one of a couple of letters in Hebrew that do not have a same sound-making letter in English.

Another word in Hebrew starting with KHET ח and makes a KHET sound is Hanukkah 'kha-noo-kah חֲנוּכָּה

KHET ח is sometimes written in English with an H or Ch. Because it makes a different sound than Ch or H, we use Kh to write it in English

Let's practice writing the letter KHET ח

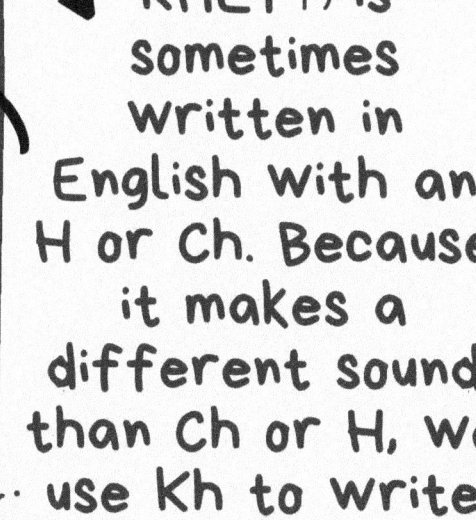

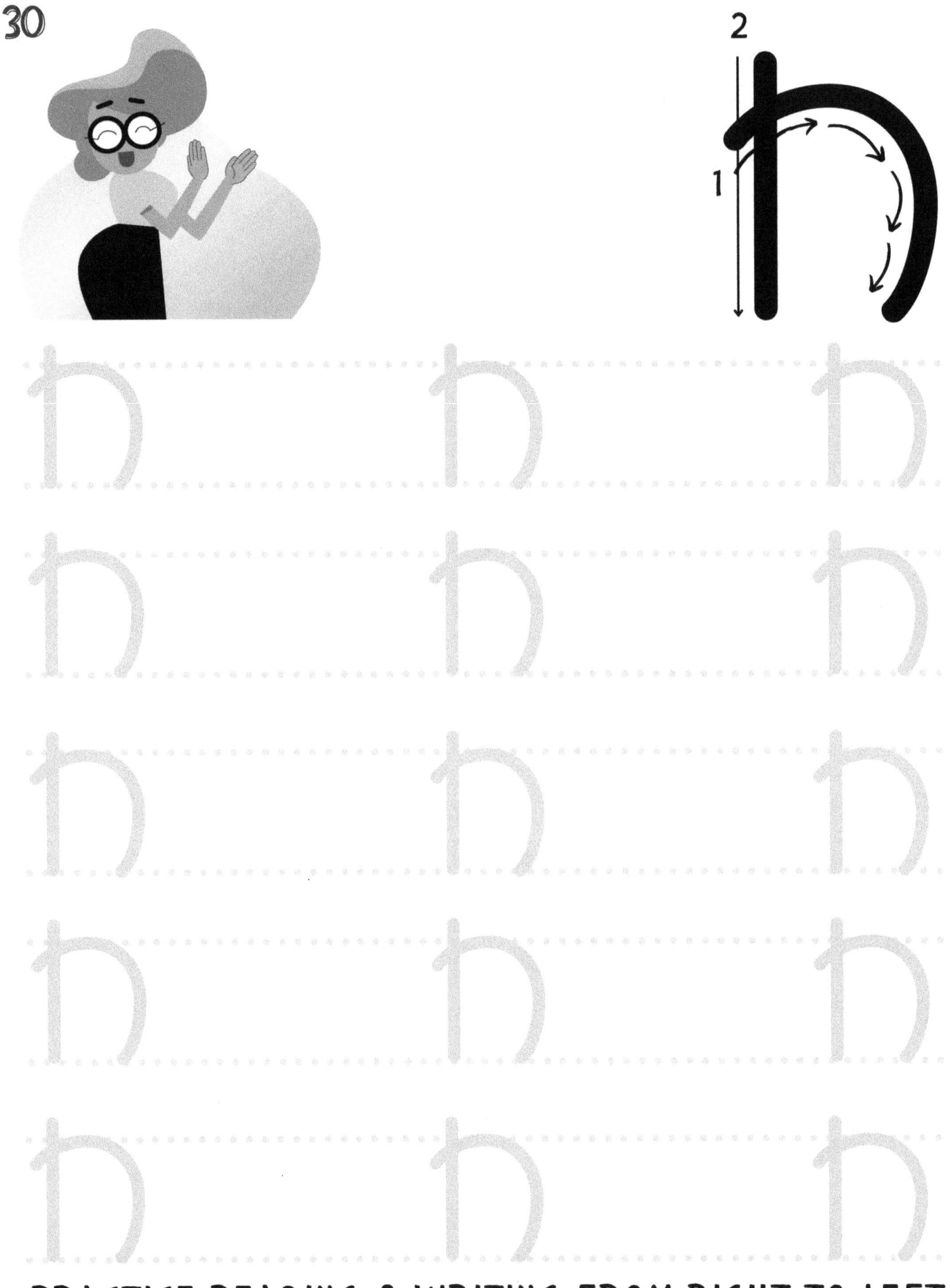

30

YOUR THIRD WORD IN HEBREW

let's put together the letters KHET and GIMEL to write the word HOLIDAY in Hebrew:

חג

Say it in Hebrew: khag

PRACTICE READING & WRITING FROM RIGHT TO LEFT

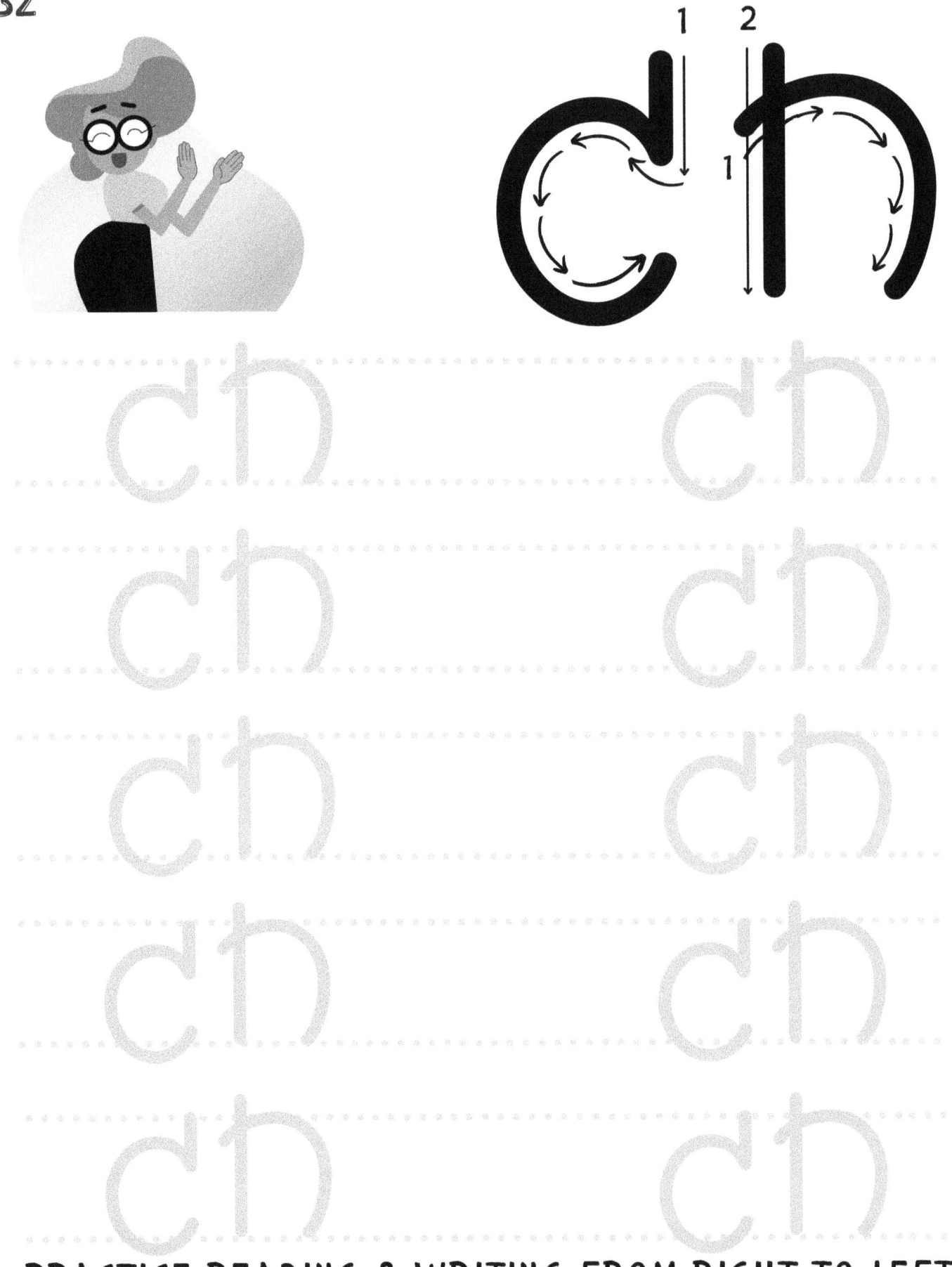

PRACTICE READING & WRITING FROM RIGHT TO LEFT

I Hope You're Loving Your Workbook

Can I ask you to invest 60 seconds in sharing your experience?
Your review is the most helpful feedback for others looking for good Hebrew resources, and for me as the author.
Toda Rabah - thank you so much!

WHERE CAN I LEAVE A REVIEW?

Great question!
You can leave a review wherever you purchased the book, or on **Google**, **Amazon**, or **Goodreads**.
Search 'Hebrew by Inbal' on any platform to leave a review.

Thank you so much again!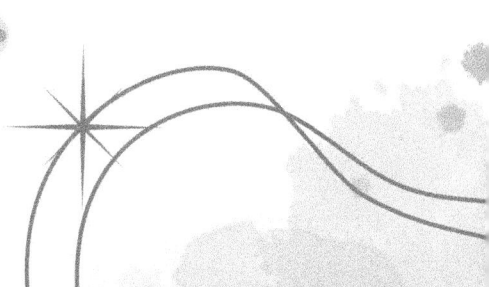

TET

tet

ט׳ת

TOASTER

טOסטׄ

'tos-ter

PRACTICE READING & WRITING FROM RIGHT TO LEFT

PRACTICE READING & WRITING FROM RIGHT TO LEFT

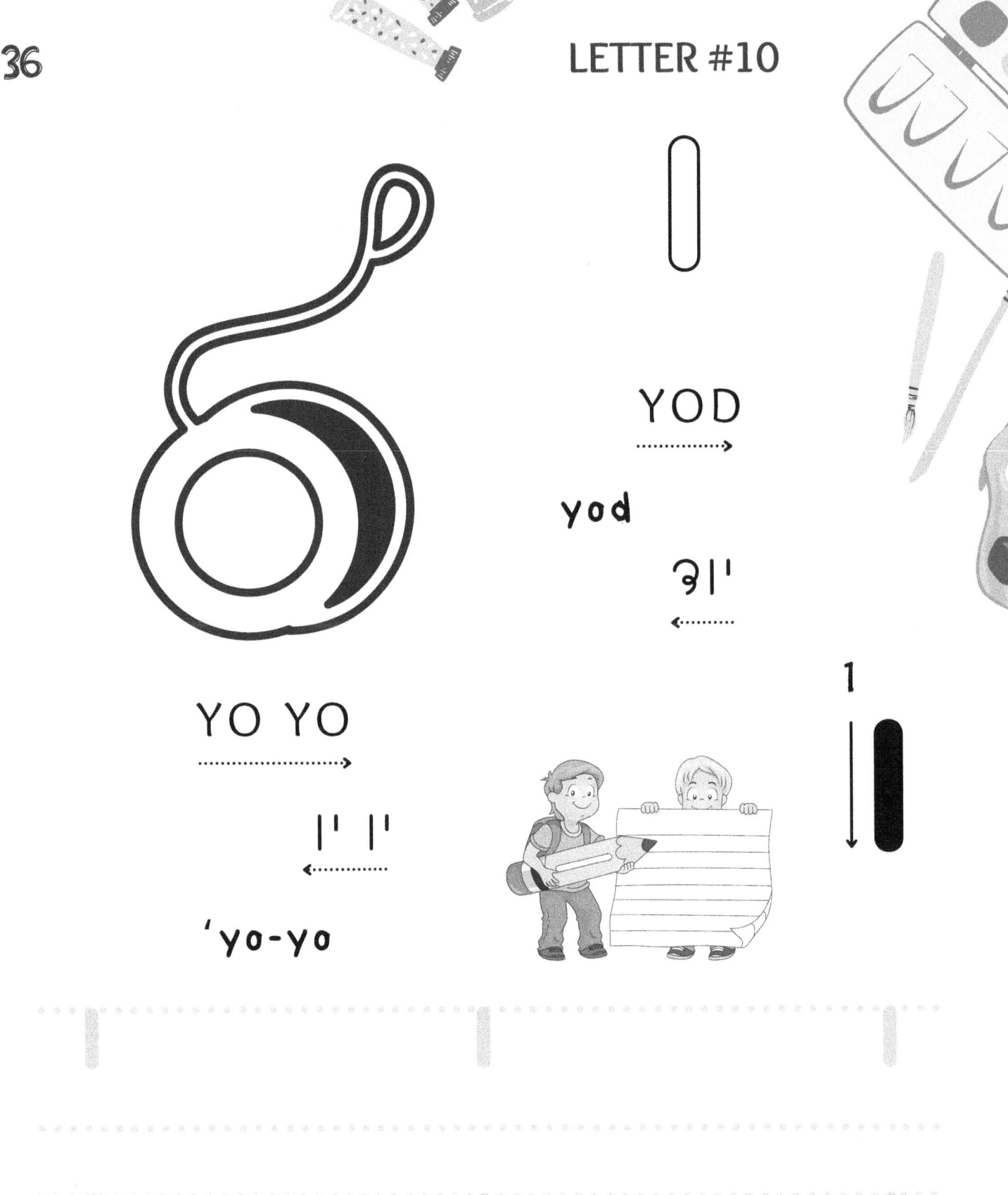

YOD

yod

ʼlɕ

YO YO

|ʼ |ʼ

ʼyo-yo

1

PRACTICE READING & WRITING FROM RIGHT TO LEFT

1

PRACTICE READING & WRITING FROM RIGHT TO LEFT

GREAT JOB! YOU ALREADY KNOW TEN LETTERS!

READ THEM IN ORDER - FROM RIGHT TO LEFT

DALET
DOLLAR

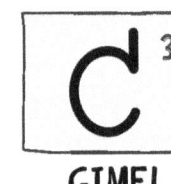

GIMEL
GUITAR

VET
(NO DOT)

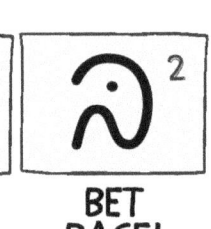

BET
BAGEL

ALEF
AMBULANCE

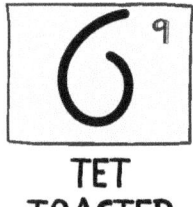

TET
TOASTER

KHET
CHALLAH

ZAYIN
ZEBRA

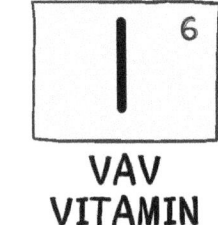

VAV
VITAMIN

HE/HEY
HI

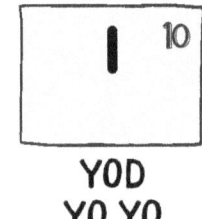

YOD
YO YO

LETTER WITH NO DUGESH (DOT REMOVED) ♡

PRACTICE YOUR LETTERS
IT'S OK TO GO BACK AND LOOK

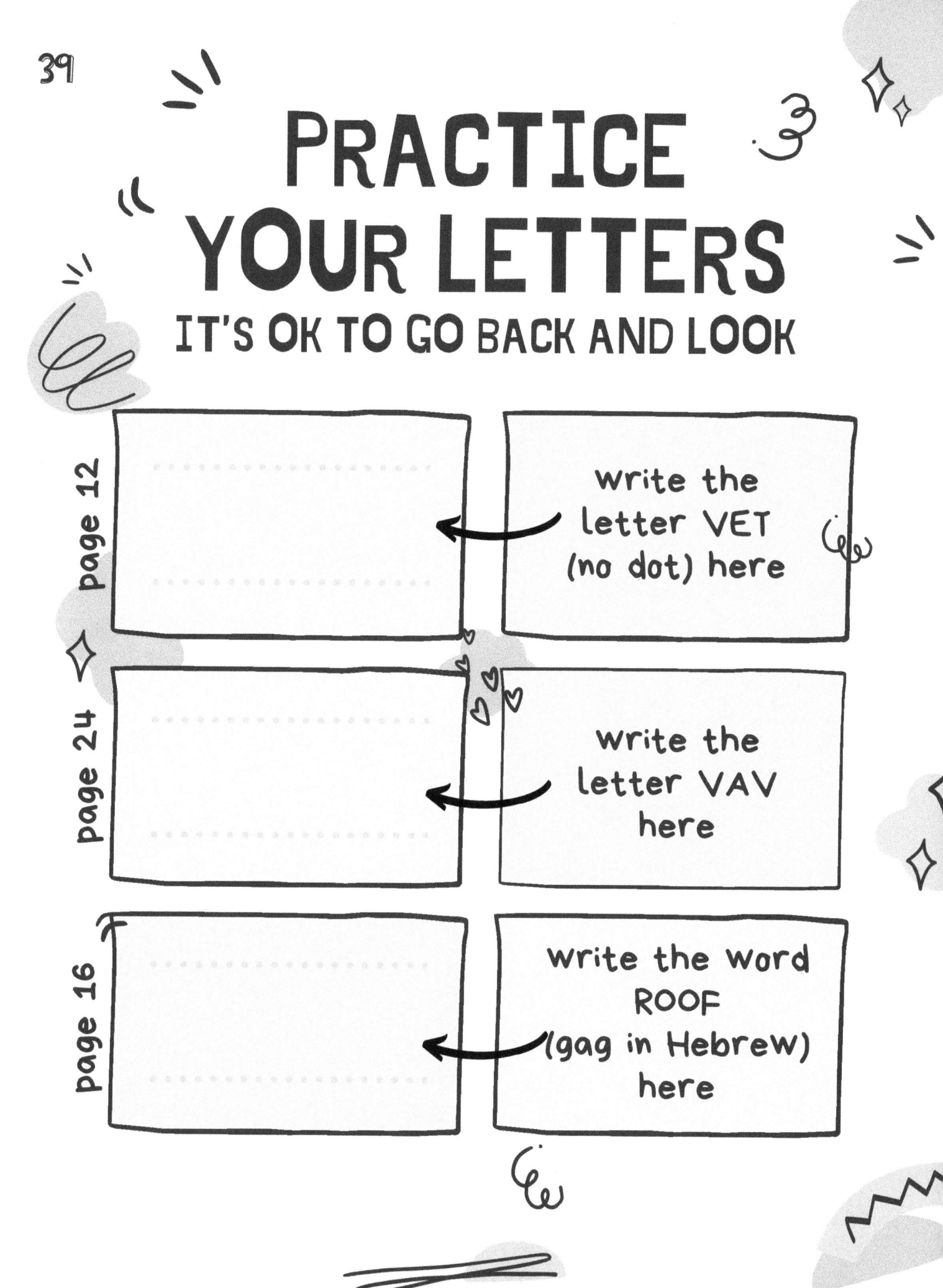

page 12

write the letter VET (no dot) here

page 24

write the letter VAV here

page 16

write the word ROOF (gag in Hebrew) here

KAF

kaf

KOSHER

ka-'sher

PRACTICE READING & WRITING FROM RIGHT TO LEFT

PRACTICE READING & WRITING FROM RIGHT TO LEFT

THINGS TO KNOW ABOUT

KAF

KAF is the second letter that has a No Dugesh variation, called KHAF

KHAF

KHAF (No Dugesh = Dot removed) makes a sound much like the letter KHET ח you already know

Because of that, KHAF כ SOUNDS like the first letter in the words Challah and Hanukkah (WRITTEN in Hebrew with a KHET ח)

Let's practice writing כ KHAF

43

KAF becomes KHAF by taking off the dot (Dugesh) in the middle. This is how we write KHAF = KAF with no Dugesh

1

PRACTICE READING & WRITING FROM RIGHT TO LEFT

THINGS TO KNOW ABOUT

ך

At the end of a word, the letter KHAF (no Dugesh = no dot) is written

KHAF at the end of a word is called KHAF SOFIT (khaf so-'feet) SOFIT is the female form of the word End

The sound of of ך KHAF does not change at the end of a word, only how it is written

We mark letters that are written different at the end of the word with a diamond

This is how
we write the
letter
כ KHAF
(No Dugesh)
at the end
of a word

LETTER #12

LAMED

'la-med

ꟼN𝄇

LAMA

'la-mah

ꝛN𝄇

PRACTICE READING & WRITING FROM RIGHT TO LEFT

PRACTICE READING & WRITING FROM RIGHT TO LEFT

YOUR NEXT WORD IN HEBREW

Now let's put together the letters LAMED and VET (no Dugesh) to write the word Heart in Hebrew:

לב

Say it in Hebrew: lev

PRACTICE READING & WRITING FROM RIGHT TO LEFT

49

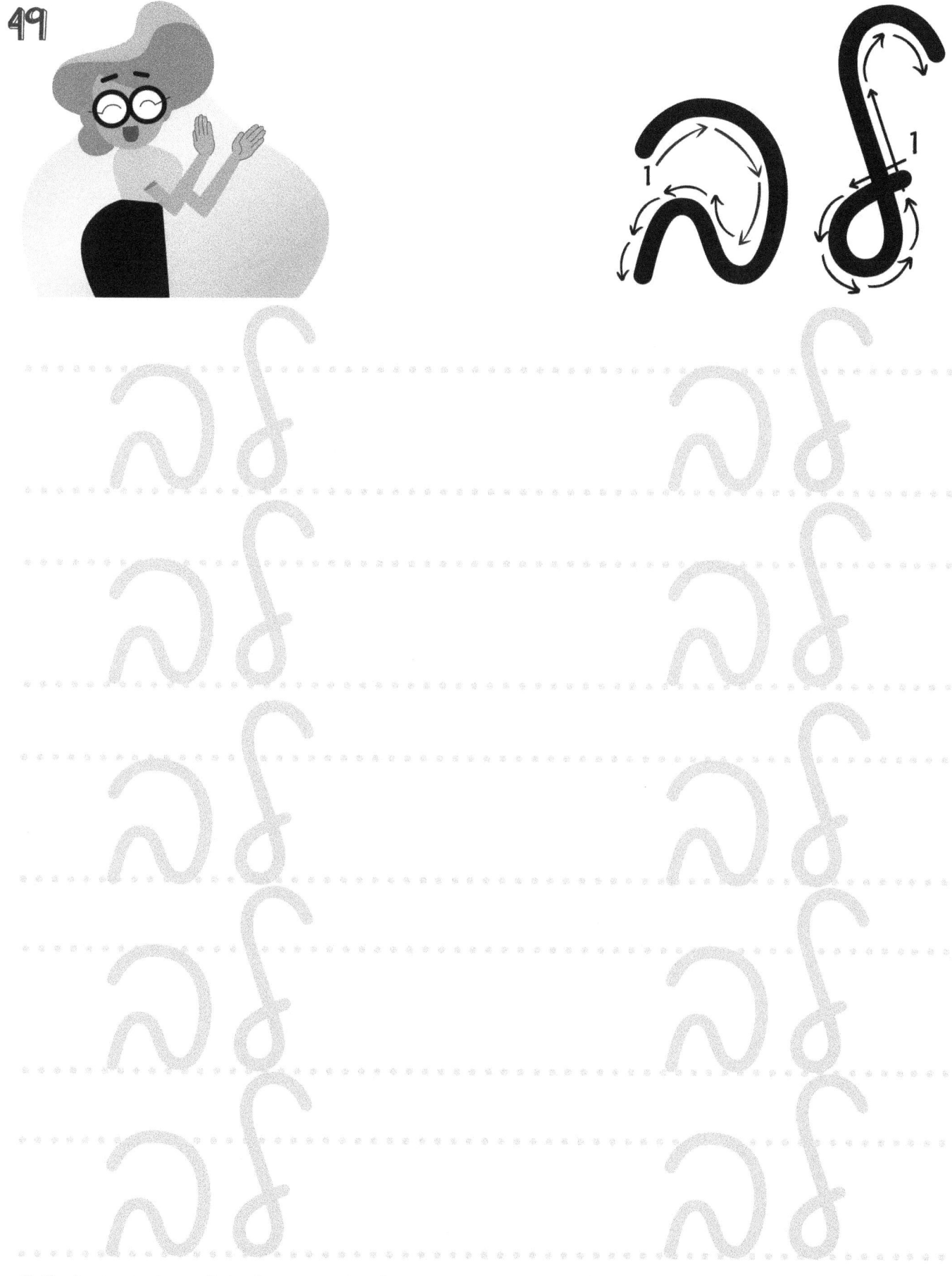

PRACTICE READING & WRITING FROM RIGHT TO LEFT

N

MEM

ᴐN   mem

MANGO

IↃJN

'man-go

1

N

N N N

N N N

PRACTICE READING & WRITING FROM RIGHT TO LEFT

PRACTICE READING & WRITING FROM RIGHT TO LEFT

THINGS TO KNOW ABOUT

N

MEM at the end of a word is written

ם

MEM at the end of a word is called MEM SOFIT (mem so-'feet)

The sound of of the the letter N MEM does not change at the end of a word, only how it is written

Let's practice writing ם

This is how
we write
the letter
N MEM
at the end
of a word

PRACTICE READING & WRITING FROM RIGHT TO LEFT

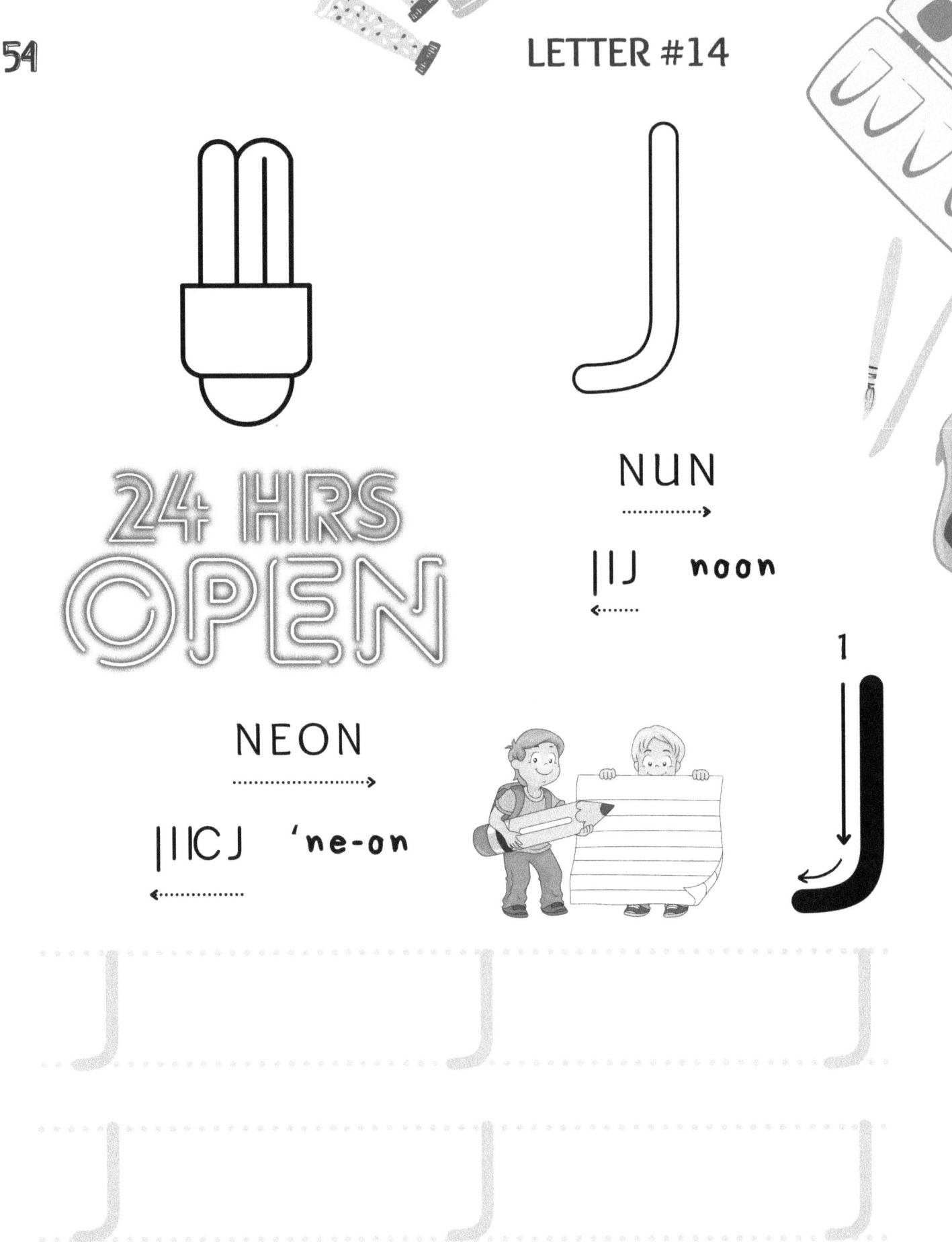

NUN

||J   noon

NEON

|||CJ   'ne-on

PRACTICE READING & WRITING FROM RIGHT TO LEFT

1

PRACTICE READING & WRITING FROM RIGHT TO LEFT

THINGS TO KNOW ABOUT

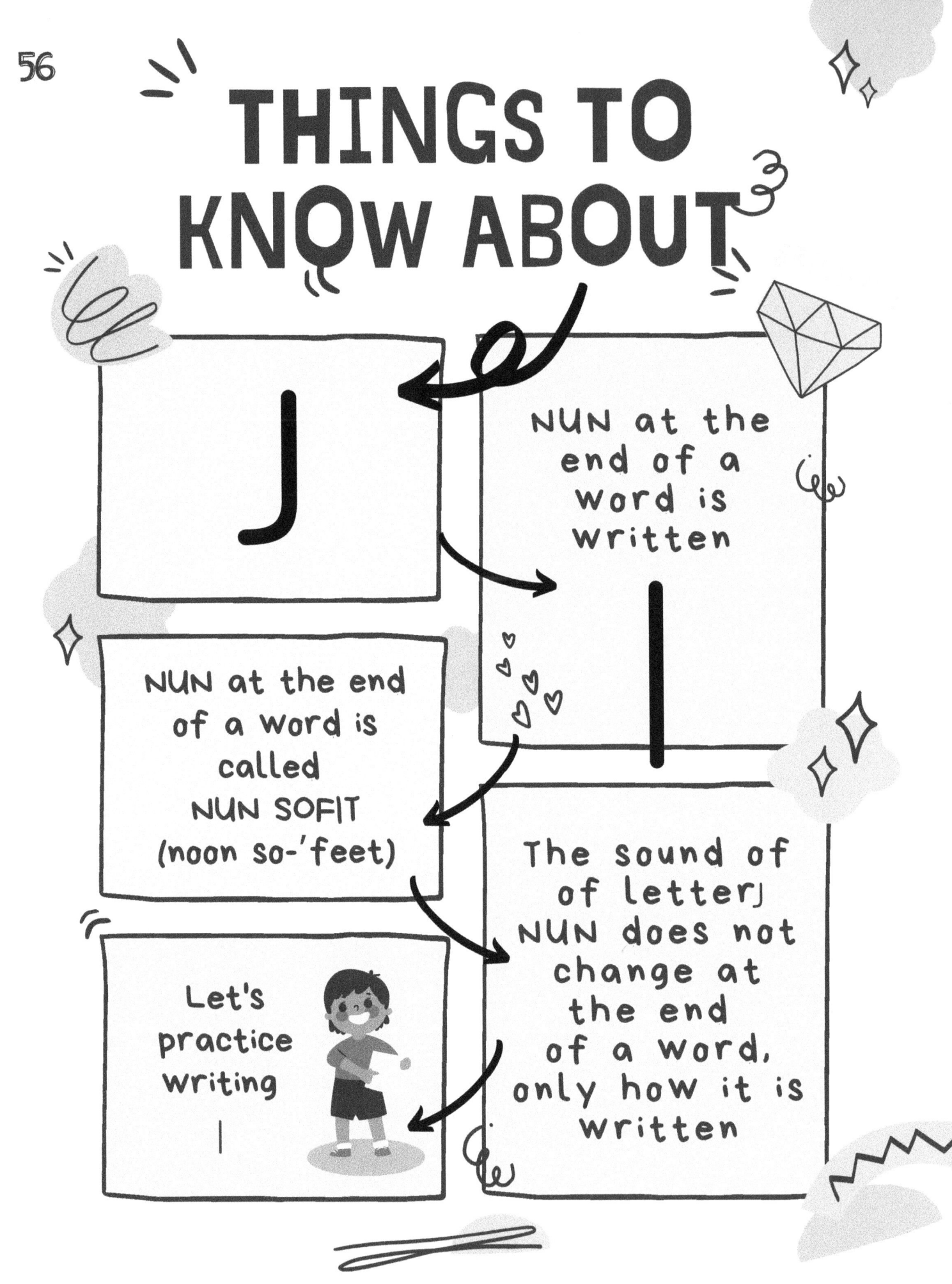

J

NUN at the end of a word is written

ן

NUN at the end of a word is called NUN SOFIT (noon so-'feet)

The sound of of letter נ NUN does not change at the end of a word, only how it is written

Let's practice writing ן

This is how we write the letter ן NUN at the end of a word

1

PRACTICE READING & WRITING FROM RIGHT TO LEFT

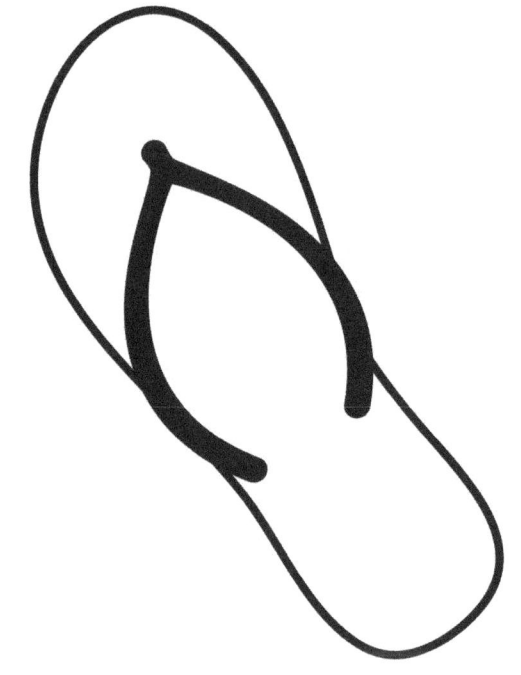

SANDAL

ס6ן

san-'dal

SAMEKH

ס6ס 'sa-mekh

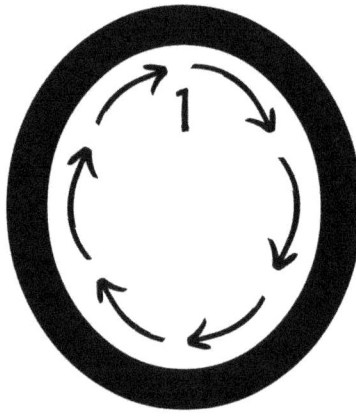

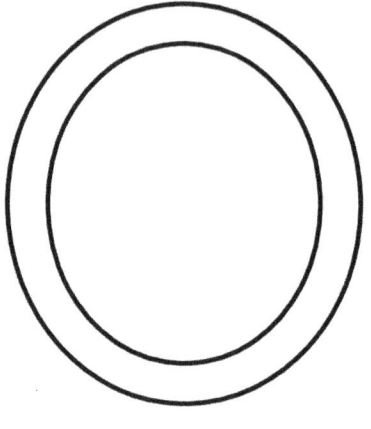

PRACTICE READING & WRITING FROM RIGHT TO LEFT

PRACTICE READING & WRITING FROM RIGHT TO LEFT

YOUR NEXT WORD IN HEBREW

Now let's put together the letters NUN and SAMEKH to write the word MIRACLE in Hebrew:

OJ

Say it in Hebrew: nes

OJ

PRACTICE READING & WRITING FROM RIGHT TO LEFT

61

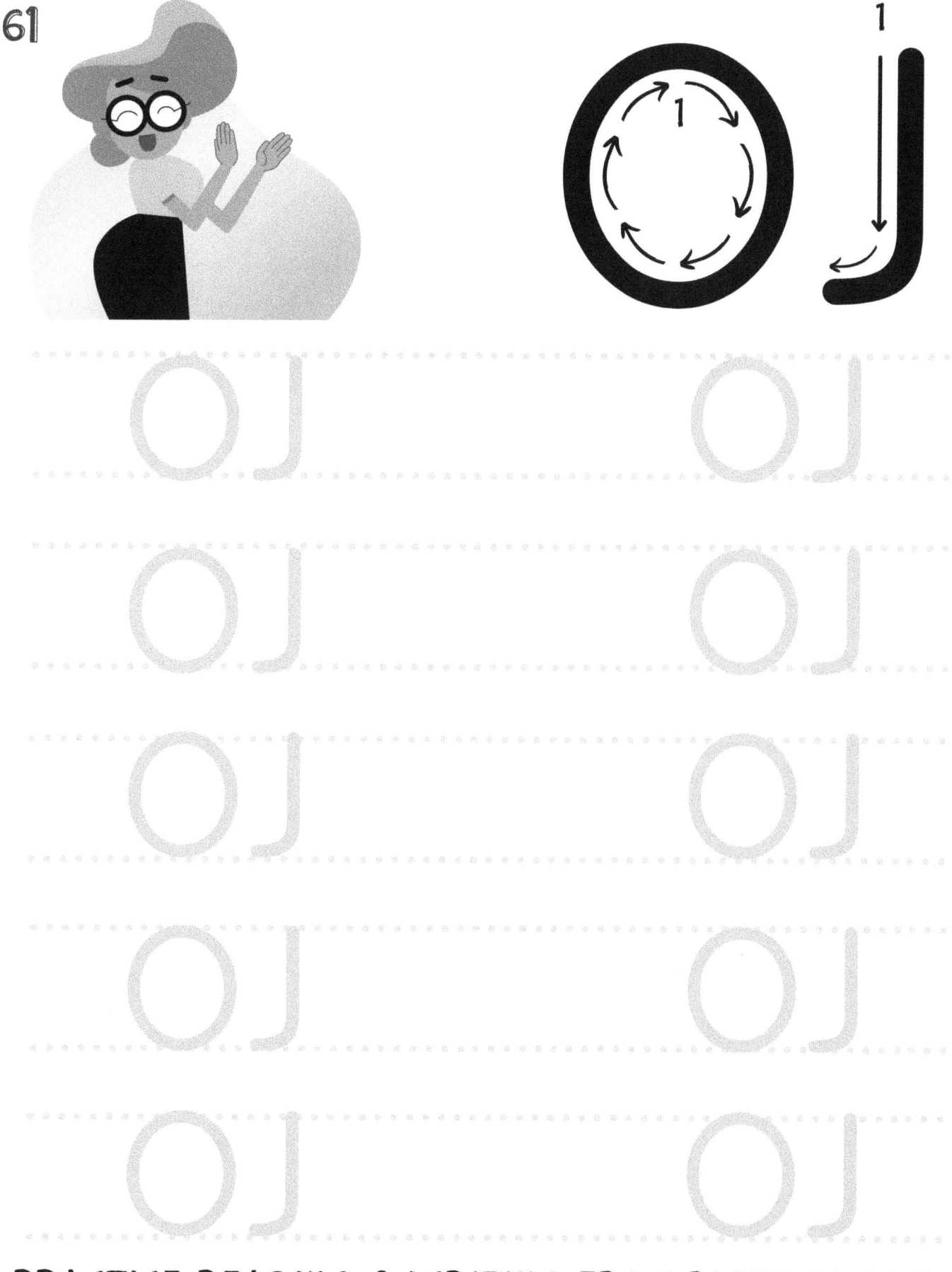

LOOK AT ALL THE LETTERS YOU KNOW!

READ THEM IN ORDER - FROM RIGHT TO LEFT

⁴ DALET DOLLAR	³ GIMEL GUITAR	VET (NO DOT)	² BET BAGEL	¹ ALEF AMBULANCE
⁹ TET TOASTER	⁸ KHET CHALLAH	⁷ ZAYIN ZEBRA	⁶ VAV VITAMIN	⁵ HE/HEY HI
¹² LAMED LAMA	(KHAF AT THE END OF A WORD)	KHAF (NO DOT)	¹¹ KAF KOSHER	¹⁰ YOD YO YO
¹⁵ SAMEKH SANDAL	(NUN AT THE END OF A WORD)	¹⁴ NUN NEON	(MEM AT THE END OF A WORD)	¹³ MEM MANGO

LETTER WITH NO DUGESH (DOT REMOVED) ♥
LETTERS AT THE END OF A WORD ◈

PRACTICE YOUR LETTERS
IT'S OK TO GO BACK AND LOOK

page 44

write the letter KHAF SOFIT here

page 58

write the letter SAMEKH here

page 48

write the word heart (lev) here

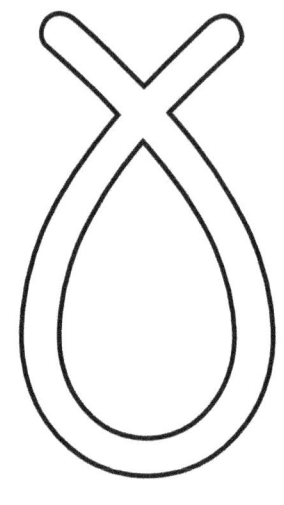

AYIN ঠ is one of
the few letters
that do not have
a same sound
making letter in
English.
That is why
we don't have a
word here.

AYIN ঠ sounds much
like the letter
ALEF IC
and you can say
them the same

AYIN

|'ঠ   'a-yeen

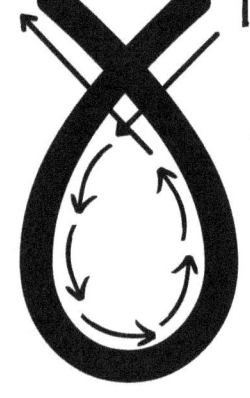

PRACTICE READING & WRITING FROM RIGHT TO LEFT

PRACTICE READING & WRITING FROM RIGHT TO LEFT

PE

pe

IC⊚

PIZZA

פּיצה

'pee-tsah

1

2

PRACTICE READING & WRITING FROM RIGHT TO LEFT

PRACTICE READING & WRITING FROM RIGHT TO LEFT

THINGS TO KNOW ABOUT

Pe

The letter PE has a variation with No Dugesh (Dot removed) called FE

Fe

FE ☺ sounds like the letter F in the word flower

PE is the third and final letter changing its sound with and without a Dugesh:

BET ♫ ♫ VET
KAF ☽ ☾ KHAF
PE ☺ ☺ FE

Let's practice writing FE ☺

69

PE becomes FE when taking off its Dugesh (dot in the middle). FE sounds like F in the word Flower

1

PRACTICE READING & WRITING FROM RIGHT TO LEFT

THINGS TO KNOW ABOUT

ॐ

FE (PE with No Dugesh) at the end of a word is written

ₓ

FE at the end of a word is called FE SOFIT. SOFIT is the feminine form of the word end.

The sound of FE ॐ does not change at the end of a word, only how it is written

Let's practice writing ₓ

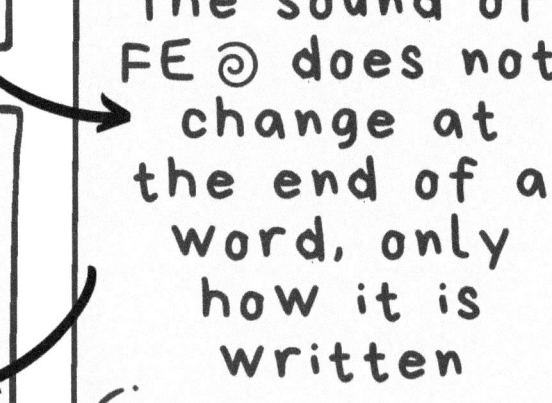

This is how
we write the
letter
FE ⊚
(No Dugesh)
at the end
of a word

PRACTICE READING & WRITING FROM RIGHT TO LEFT

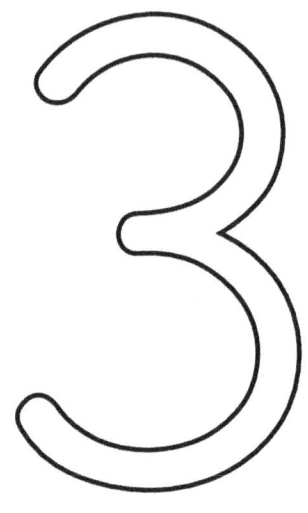

TSADI is the final letter that does not have a same sound-making letter in English. That is why we don't have a word here.

TSADI makes a TS sound like the z in the word Pizza

'tsa-dee   TSADI

·········>

'צ3

<·········

3 3 3

3 3 3

PRACTICE READING & WRITING FROM RIGHT TO LEFT

PRACTICE READING & WRITING FROM RIGHT TO LEFT

THINGS TO KNOW ABOUT

3

TSADI 3 at the end of a word is written ץ

TSADI 3 at the end of a word is called
TSADI SOFIT
('tsa-dee so-'feet)

The sound of TSADI 3 at the end of a word does not change, only how it is written

Let's practice writing ץ

This is how
we write the
letter
TSADI
at the end
of a word

PRACTICE READING & WRITING FROM RIGHT TO LEFT

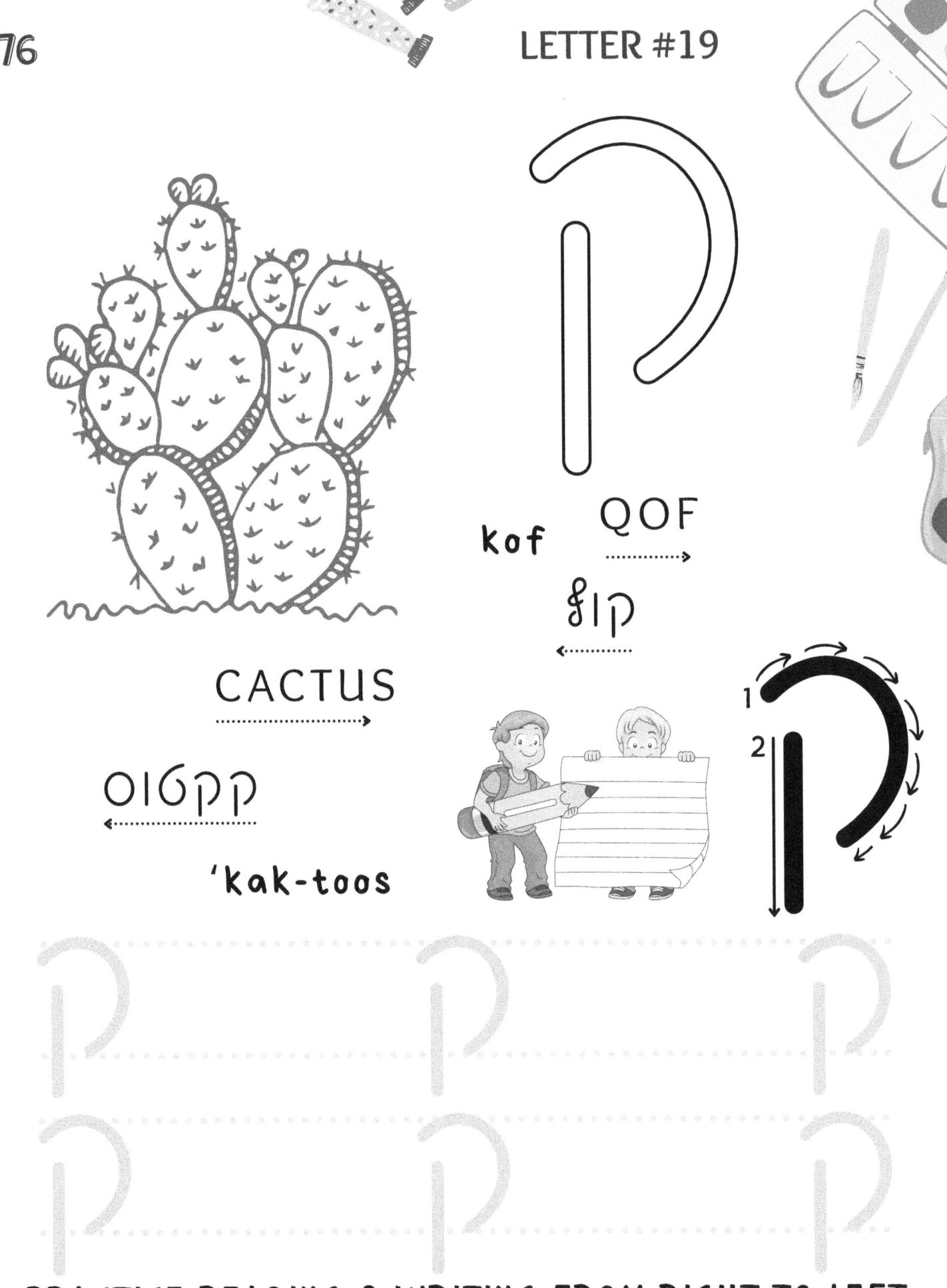

kof

QOF
·····▸

ϛιρ
◂·····

CACTUS
·····▸

οιϛρρ
◂·····

'kak-toos

1
2

PRACTICE READING & WRITING FROM RIGHT TO LEFT

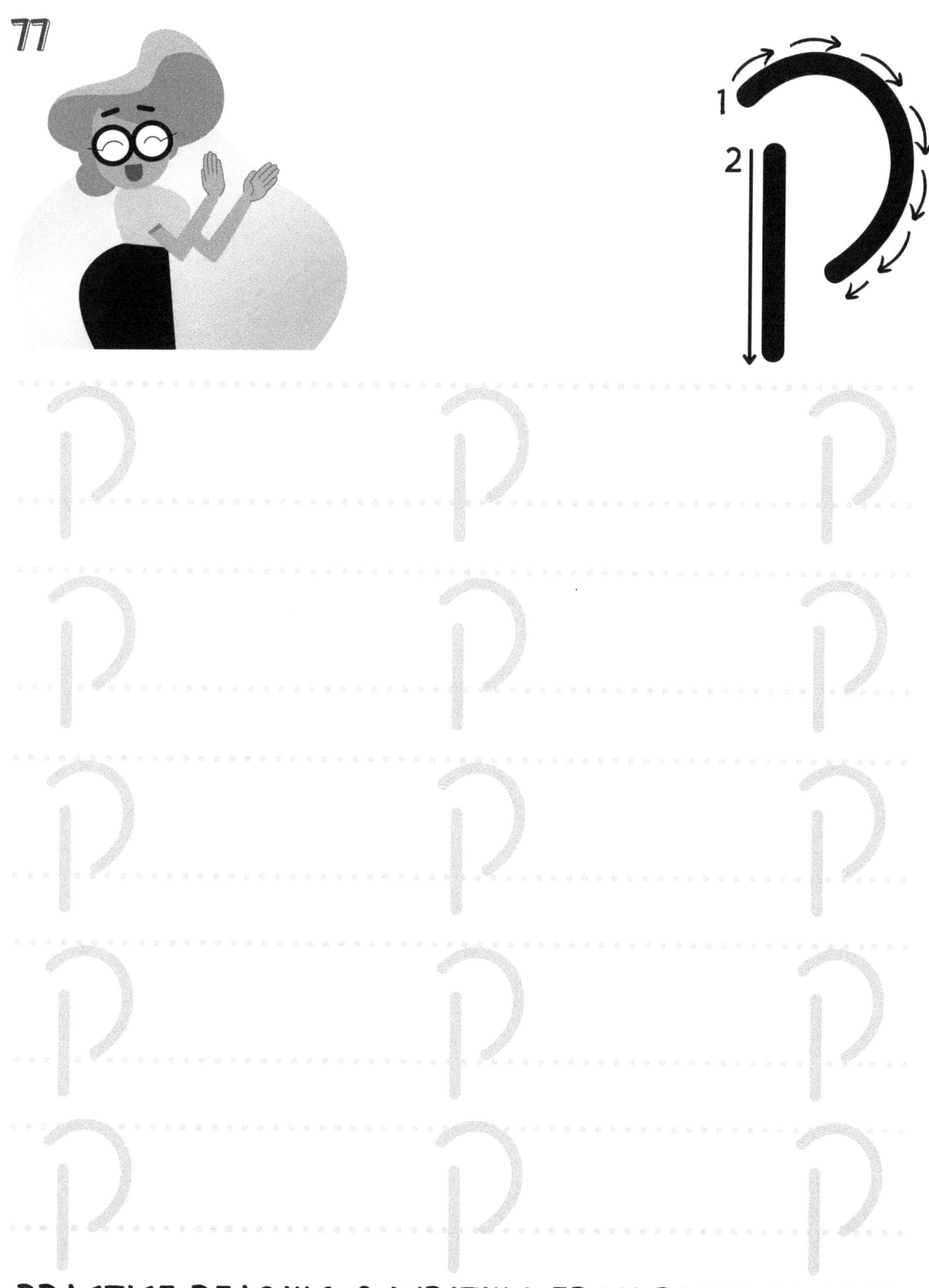

PRACTICE READING & WRITING FROM RIGHT TO LEFT

RESH

ϱ׳ך　resh

ROLLERBLADES

אגַ׳׳רלַבֿרֿ‎ן　'ro-ler-b-leyd-s

1

PRACTICE READING & WRITING FROM RIGHT TO LEFT

PRACTICE READING & WRITING FROM RIGHT TO LEFT

SHIN

sheen   ا' ﻋ

SHHHH....

....ééé

sh....

PRACTICE READING & WRITING FROM RIGHT TO LEFT

SHIN ℮ with a dot on the top right corner makes a SH sound. This is how we write it

PRACTICE READING & WRITING FROM RIGHT TO LEFT

THINGS TO KNOW ABOUT

ℓ̇ SHIN

SHIN becomes SIN by moving the dot from the right top corner to the left

ℓ̇ SIN

SIN (seen) ℓ makes an S sound, just like the letter SAMEKH ○ you learned

Unlike the dots in the middle in the letters BET, KAF, and PE, called Dugesh, the dot in the letters SHIN and SIN is not called a Dugesh

SHIN (sheen) is called Right-sided SHIN, and SIN is called left-sided SHIN, based on where the dot is placed.

SIN ℮ with a dot on the top left corner makes an S sound. This is how we write it

PRACTICE READING & WRITING FROM RIGHT TO LEFT

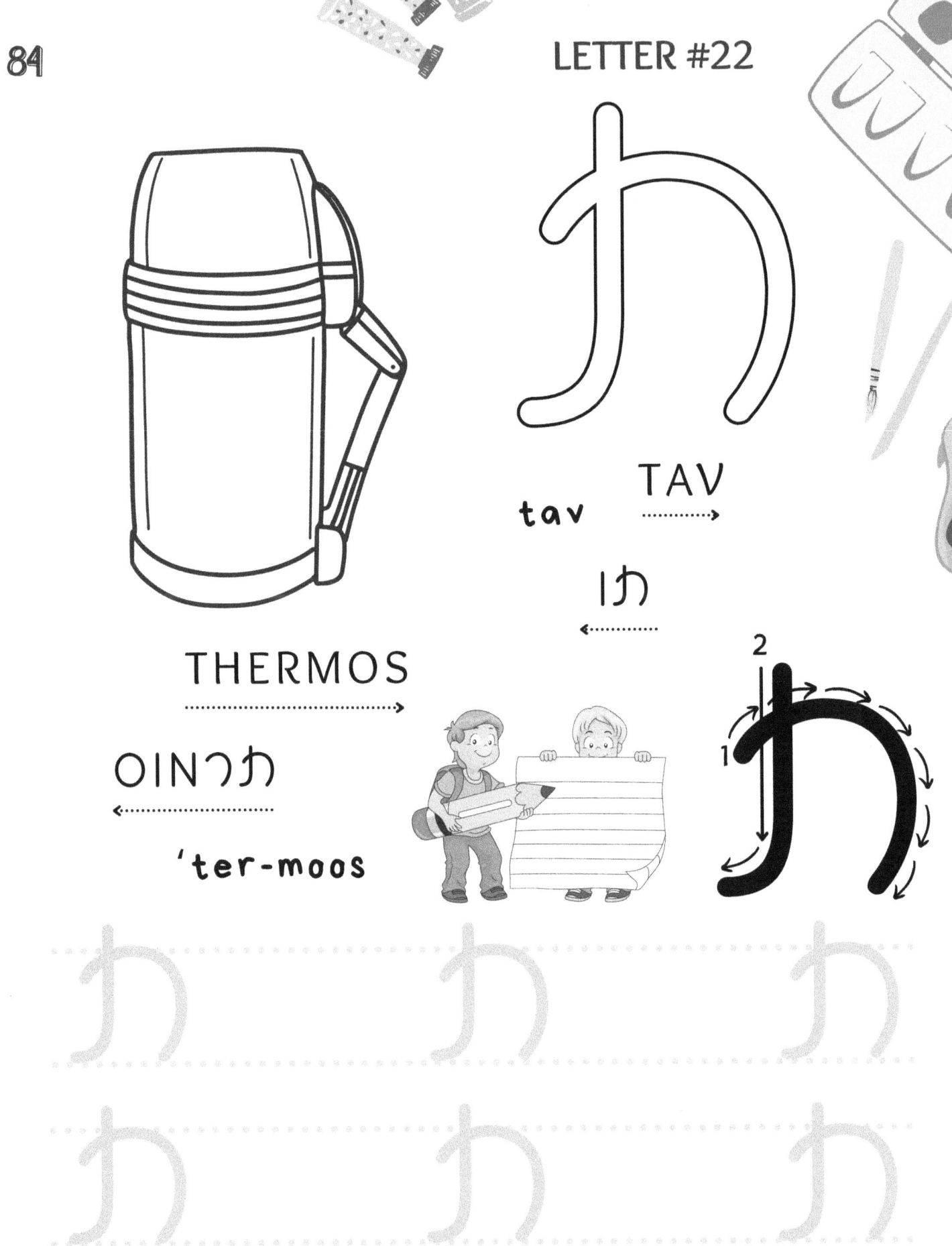

TAV

tav

THERMOS

OINつカ

'ter-moos

PRACTICE READING & WRITING FROM RIGHT TO LEFT

85

PRACTICE READING & WRITING FROM RIGHT TO LEFT

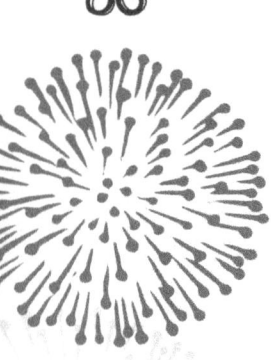

YOUR NEXT WORD IN HEBREW

Now let's put together the letters SHIN (dot on the right top corner), BET (with a Dugesh) and TAV to write the word Saturday in Hebrew:

שַׁבָּת

Say it in Hebrew: sha-'bat

PRACTICE READING & WRITING FROM RIGHT TO LEFT

PRACTICE READING & WRITING FROM RIGHT TO LEFT

YOU KNOW THE ENTIRE ALPHABET!

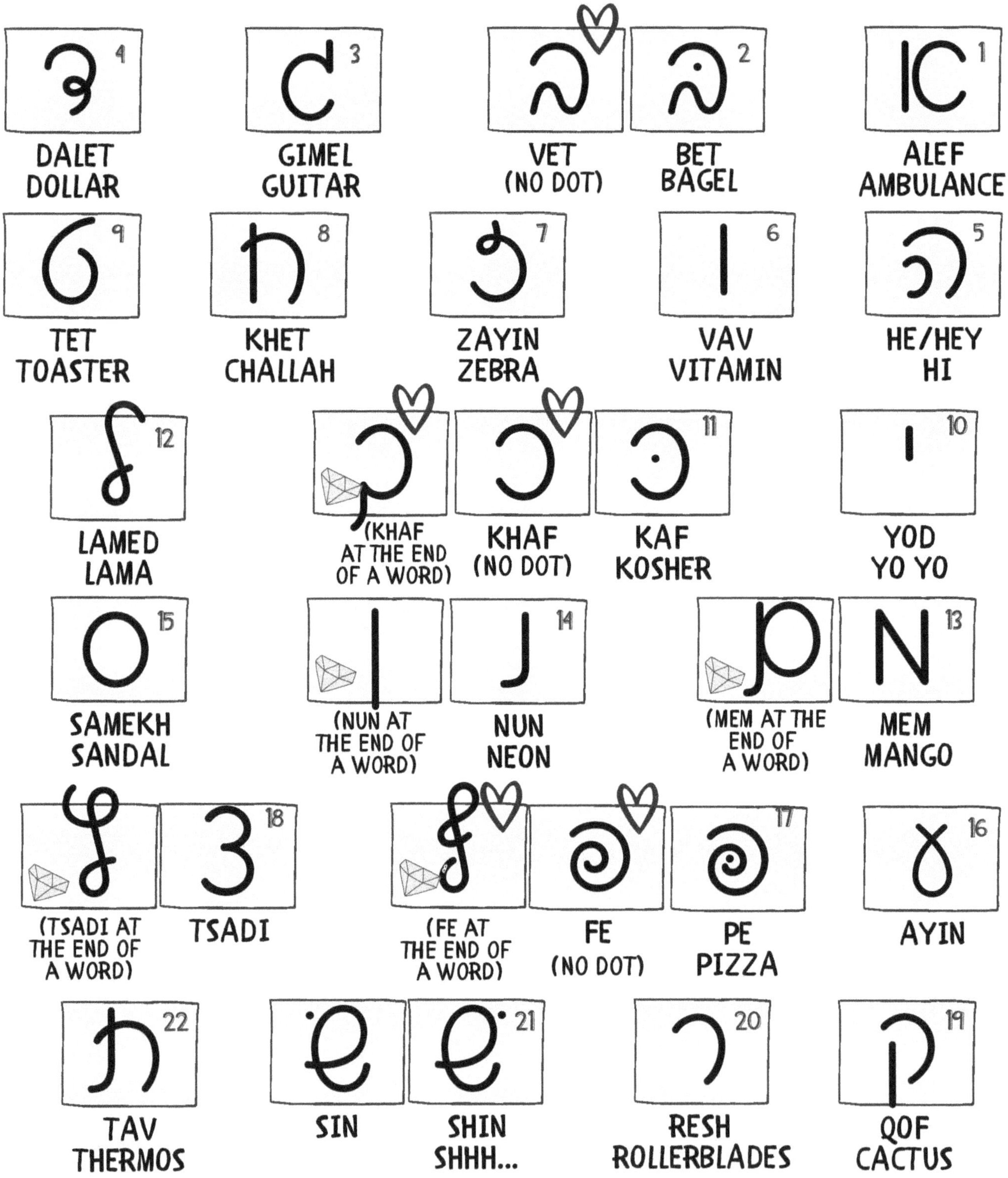

ᴅ⁴	ᴄ³	ב ♡ / ב²		IC¹
DALET **DOLLAR**	**GIMEL** **GUITAR**	**VET** **(NO DOT)** / **BET** **BAGEL**		**ALEF** **AMBULANCE**

ᴛᴇᴛ⁹	ᴋʜᴇᴛ⁸	ᴢᴀʏɪɴ⁷	ᴠᴀᴠ⁶	ʜᴇ⁵
TET **TOASTER**	**KHET** **CHALLAH**	**ZAYIN** **ZEBRA**	**VAV** **VITAMIN**	**HE/HEY** **HI**

¹²	♡ / ♡ / ⊙¹¹		¹⁰
LAMED **LAMA**	**(KHAF AT THE END OF A WORD)** / **KHAF (NO DOT)** / **KAF KOSHER**		**YOD** **YO YO**

O¹⁵	¹⁴ / J¹⁴		JON / N¹³
SAMEKH **SANDAL**	**(NUN AT THE END OF A WORD)** / **NUN NEON**		**(MEM AT THE END OF A WORD)** / **MEM MANGO**

/ 3¹⁸	♡ / ♡ /	¹⁷	¹⁶
(TSADI AT THE END OF A WORD) / **TSADI**	**(FE AT THE END OF A WORD)** / **FE (NO DOT)** / **PE PIZZA**		**AYIN**

ה²²	e / e²¹	⊃²⁰	ᴩ¹⁹
TAV **THERMOS**	**SIN** / **SHIN SHHH...**	**RESH** **ROLLERBLADES**	**QOF** **CACTUS**

LETTER WITH NO DUGESH (DOT REMOVED) ♡
LETTERS AT THE END OF A WORD ◈

PRACTICE YOUR LETTERS
IT'S OK TO GO BACK AND LOOK

page 64

write the letter AYIN here

page 82

write the letter SIN (dot on the left corner) here

page 86

write the word Saturday (sha-bat in Hebrew) here

PRACTICE YOUR LETTERS
IT'S OK TO GO BACK AND LOOK

page 14

write the letter GIMEL here

page 36

write the letter YOD here

page 60

write the word miracle (nes) here

YOU KNOW THE ENTIRE ALPHABET!

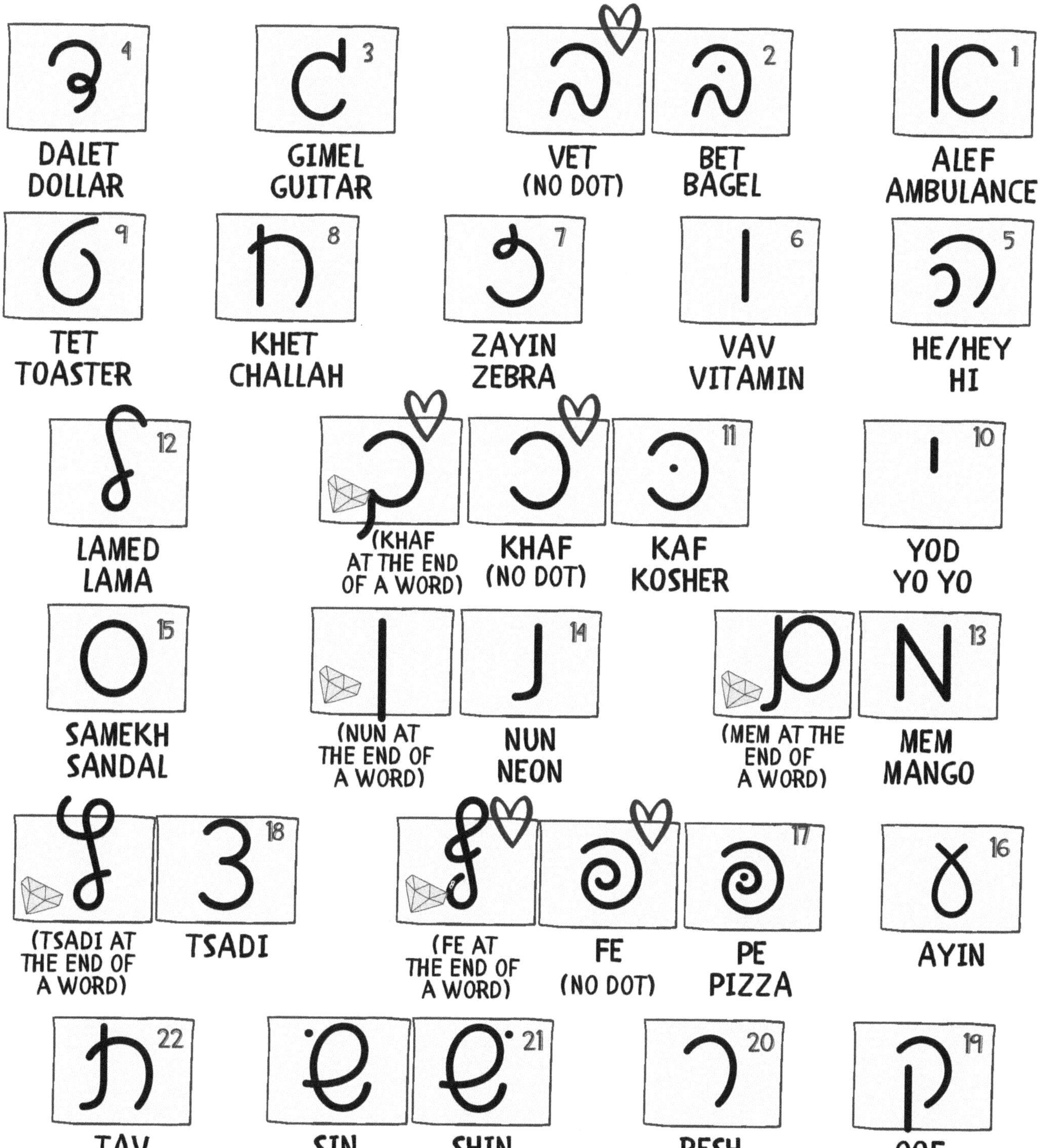

DALET DOLLAR [4]

GIMEL GUITAR [3]

VET (NO DOT)

BET BAGEL [2]

ALEF AMBULANCE [1]

TET TOASTER [9]

KHET CHALLAH [8]

ZAYIN ZEBRA [7]

VAV VITAMIN [6]

HE/HEY HI [5]

LAMED LAMA [12]

(KHAF AT THE END OF A WORD)

KHAF (NO DOT)

KAF KOSHER [11]

YOD YO YO [10]

SAMEKH SANDAL [15]

(NUN AT THE END OF A WORD)

NUN NEON [14]

(MEM AT THE END OF A WORD)

MEM MANGO [13]

(TSADI AT THE END OF A WORD)

TSADI [18]

(FE AT THE END OF A WORD)

FE (NO DOT)

PE PIZZA [17]

AYIN [16]

TAV THERMOS [22]

SIN

SHIN SHHH... [21]

RESH ROLLERBLADES [20]

QOF CACTUS [19]

LETTER WITH NO DUGESH (DOT REMOVED) ♡
LETTERS AT THE END OF A WORD ◇

THIS PAGE IS BLANK
SO YOU CAN CUT-OUT
THE ALPHABET SHEET AT THE BACK OF THIS PAGE.

MOUNT IT ON THE WALL,
CARRY IT WITH YOU ON-THE-GO,
OR BRING IT TO CLASS FOR QUICK & EASY ACCESS

YOU DID IT – CONGRATULATIONS!

You've just crossed the second finish line in your Hebrew reading and writing journey — and what an achievement it is!

By completing this workbook, you've mastered the Cursive Script Alphabet — a skill that ensures you can confidently handle anything in Hebrew, whether it's in Print or Cursive.

I hope you're feeling incredibly proud of yourself, because I'm cheering for you all the way!

THE BIG PICTURE

This is a huge step, and you only have one more step to complete all your reading and writing skills. When you complete Hebrew 1, 2, and 3, everything will click into place - you'll see! ☺

YOUR NEXT STEP:

Start Hebrew 3 — the final step! Here, you'll master the vowel (Nikud) system, complete your reading skills, and bring everything together now that you've nailed your writing skills in Hebrew 1 and 2.

If you haven't ordered your copy of Hebrew 3 yet, find the best place to grab yours at hebrewbyinbal.com/order.

I'M HERE FOR YOU

If you have questions or need advice about Hebrew 2, don't hesitate to reach out — I'm just a click away inside the free course.

SHARE YOUR SUCCESS

It would mean the world to me if you could take 60 seconds and leave a review of Hebrew 2 (and Hebrew 1 if you haven't already) on Amazon, Google, Goodreads, or wherever you purchased the workbook. Your feedback is the best gift you can give others starting their Hebrew journey, and me as the author.

Thank you for letting me be part of your journey. I can't wait to see you in Hebrew 3 — you're so close to the finish line!

Inbal Amit

PRACTICE READING & WRITING FROM RIGHT TO LEFT

PRACTICE READING & WRITING FROM RIGHT TO LEFT

PRACTICE READING & WRITING FROM RIGHT TO LEFT

PRACTICE READING & WRITING FROM RIGHT TO LEFT

PRACTICE READING & WRITING FROM RIGHT TO LEFT